A LIFE OF LOVE

PLANNING TO PROTECT YOUR ANIMAL FOR THE LENGTH OF ITS LIFE, NOT YOURS

A LIFE OF LOVE

PLANNING TO PROTECT YOUR ANIMAL
FOR THE LENGTH OF <u>ITS</u> LIFE, NOT <u>YOURS</u>

Learn how to guarantee your beloved animal's safety and
protection in the event that something happens to you.

AJ Fudge
Attorney

For information contact:
Law Offices of AJ Fudge
www.ajfudge.com
www.lawofficesofajfudge.com
aj@lawofficesofajfudge.com

ISBN: 978-0-9973949-0-0 (paperback)
ISBN: 978-0-9973949-1-7 (e-book)
ISBN: 978-0-9973949-2-4 (digital)

Library of Congress Control Number: 2016905119
Law Offices of AJ Fudge, Los Osos, California

Acknowledgements

First, and foremost, thank you to my true love and partner for life, Travis, for all of the unconditional love, support, and inspiration that you are always there to provide me. Thank you to all of my animals for their love, compassion, and companionship. They are my angels. Thank you to my given family for their long-time love and support, to my friend Kendra for her valuable input, and to all of the organizations and individuals that work so hard to make this world a better place for us all.

For Twink and all those like her.

TABLE OF CONTENTS

ADDITIONAL CONSIDERATIONS
49

ANIMALS & THE LAW TODAY
56

WHAT HAPPENED TO TWINK?
62

Who is Twink?

At this point, you may be asking, "Who in the world is Twink?"

Well, in the words of an advertisement on the Santa Maria Valley Humane Society's website, this is who Twink is:

Twink! AKA TWINKY DINK!
Awww, take a look at this sweet little girl. She just hasn't been the same since her only owner passed away and is looking for someone to fill up that hole in her heart. So much love to give, this mellow twelve year old rat terrier mix just wants to lounge around and give you company. She is a sucker for treats, too! We found Twink doesn't seem to be a fan of children, we think she would be ideal for an older person. She is excellent company, enjoys car rides, walks and just hanging out. Are you looking for a good listener, a constant companion, loyalty, someone to hang out with on movie night? Come in and meet Twink. She is waiting for you!

As I write these words, Twink is still at the shelter, where she's been waiting for **5 months and 27 days**. Is this where she will spend her final days after having a loving home for 12 years?

It breaks my heart to think of Twink, and the thousands like her. This poor dog lost her owner of 12 years, lost her home, and for almost six months she has endured life at a shelter, which may be the last home she ever knows. It is some consolation to know that she is at a "no-kill" shelter. However, when I think about her situation and all she's gone through, it is very frustrating. It could have easily been prevented.

Twink is a wonderful example of why I am so passionate about spreading the word to animal lovers that you need to plan to protect your animal. Otherwise, your animal could end up like Twink, or worse, and believe me, sadly it does get worse.

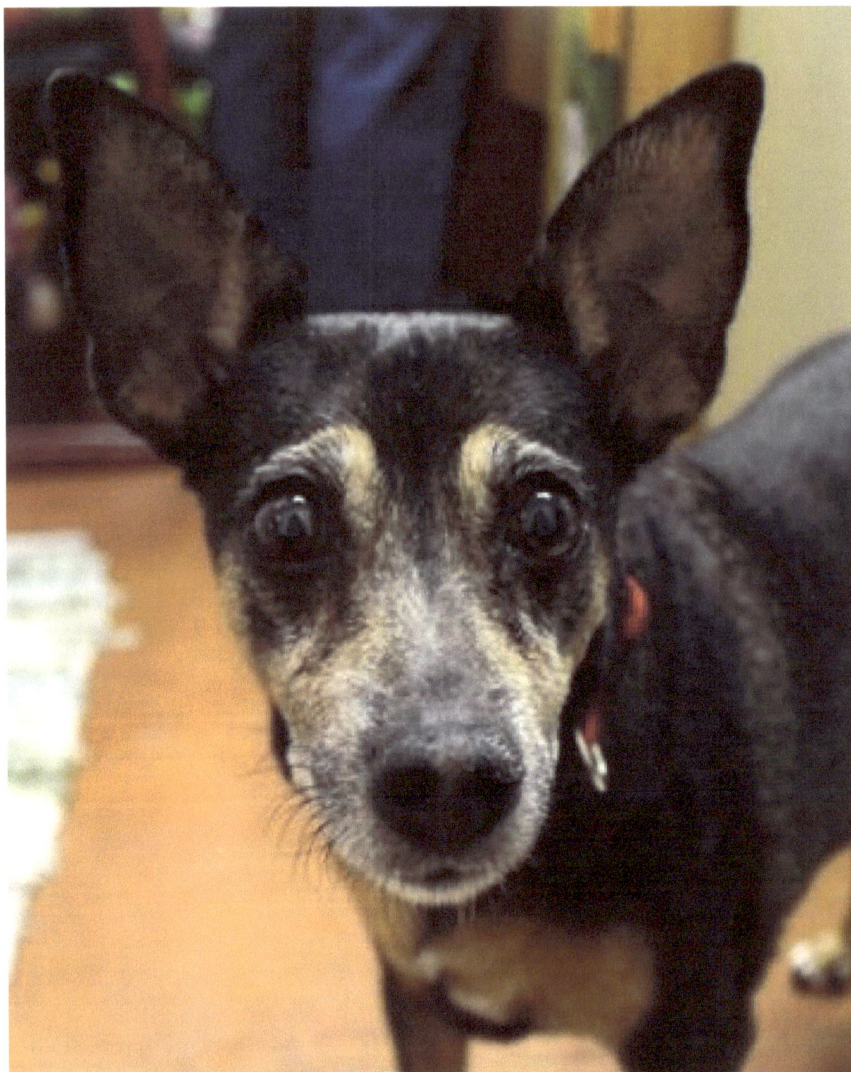

Twink at the Santa Maria Valley Humane Society in 2015

That leads me to the central question of this book: are you committed to caring for your animal for your entire life or for your animal's entire life?

This is an important distinction, and as you can see, it can have life or death consequences for your animal.

When you bring an animal into your life, you most likely do so believing that you will be with them until the end. You know that ultimately, one day, your animal will pass away. If you've had animals before, then you know the unique pain and loss you feel when an animal passes away. Yet it feels comforting to know that you gave your faithful companion love, safety, and security for its entire life. You made sure your animal was never homeless, never in a shelter, and never labeled unwanted and euthanized. Of course you are heartbroken when you lose an animal, but it feels good to know that you protected them from the harsh realities of our times that no animal deserves to face.

The most important message of this book is that the pain you suffer from losing your animal is nothing compared to the pain your animal could suffer without you and without the proper planning.

This bring us to another question, what do words like "love" and "commitment" really mean when talking about loving your animal and being committed to taking care of it for its entire life?

If I were to ask you, "Are you committed to taking care of your animal for its entire life?" You would probably answer "yes", but your answer is probably based on at least one very large assumption. Namely, that you will outlive your animal, and that you will always be able to take care of your animal. But what if you're not? What if something happens to you? What happens to your animal? Is your animal left on its own? Are you naively hoping that family or friends will step in? Uncertainty can be tragic for your animal. True love and commitment means having a plan.

Most of us would shudder at the thought of our beloved animal fending for itself or having its fate left to chance like Twink. Yet, we have not taken any action to actually prevent this from happening. In reality, we are operating as though we have a crystal ball and are 100% certain that we will outlive our animals. I'm sure Twink's owner really loved her, and never wanted anything bad to happen to her. She probably assumed she would outlive Twink, or if not, that her family or friends would take care of Twink. The reality is that it is almost six months later, and Twink is still spending nights alone at the shelter. Twink is not feeling the love or commitment, and that's because Twink's owner needed a back-up plan for Twink. When it comes to an animal, a true lifetime of love and commitment requires a bit of planning.

Outliving our animals is the ideal plan for all of us, but as you'll see throughout this book, I'm all about the back-up plan. It is always better to have a back-up plan in place than to do nothing, and this couldn't be more important or true when it comes to our animals. Much like young children, they rely on us to take care of them in every way, and it's actually quite easy to do some basic planning to protect them. That's the whole point of this book: to encourage you to take action to keep your loving animal out of the local shelter or worse. It can happen faster than you think if you don't plan ahead.

So, next question, have you ever really thought about what would happen to your animal if something were to happen to you? Have you given this important matter the time and attention that it deserves? Do you understand the importance of having a legally binding plan in place? It is time to face the reality of what could happen to your beloved animal if something happens to you. Then you will start to see how incredibly crucial it is to have a comprehensive plan in place to make sure your animal is protected. It may require some time and expense on your part, but your efforts will be rewarded tenfold. In the end you will feel a tremendous relief knowing that your animal will continue living a happy life even if you are no longer around.

Sadly, many people choose to live in denial when it comes to this subject. It can be difficult for some to face mortality and do the necessary planning. Instead, they do nothing and tell themselves that a family member or friend will certainly do the right thing. The heartbreaking result is that every day there are loving animals facing a tragic end to their lives. These situations could have easily been avoided if their owner had done a bit of simple planning. As we all know, without a loving home, animals face a world where the odds are stacked against them. No animal lover ever thinks this will happen to their animal, but it does, over and over again.

We have all heard tear-jerking stories like Twink's. Unfortunately, a very common reason that animals end up at the shelter is that something has happened to the animal's owner, and none of the family or friends are willing or able to take the animal. After all, animals are a responsibility; they require time, attention, and money. In the moment of need, often there is no one who is willing and/or able to accept such a responsibility. Casual conversations and assurances are clearly not enough to get it done. You need to have a solid plan in place.

Another challenge facing animals is the issue of how animals are treated under the law, which we will touch on more throughout the book. Suffice it to say that for estate planning purposes, animals are treated no differently than any other item of property such as a book or a chair. This has some very serious consequences for animals that most people are not even aware of. Ignorance may be bliss for you, but in this case it can be a nightmare for your animal.

Our animals are like children in that they depend on us to take care of them. However, in most cases, our children grow up into independent adults who can take care of themselves. This is not the case with our animals. No matter their age or life expectancy, our animals literally depend on us to protect and care for them. Thus, in the event that something unexpected happens to us, we need to make sure our animal's care and protection continues without interruption or uncertainty.

Perhaps, one day we will see a world where animals are cherished, respected, and treated like the benevolent souls they most certainly are. As Bob Dylan once said, "The times they are a changin'," and for the animals, the change appears to be moving in that direction. Until we get there, we must continue to support the movement, and do everything we can to ensure the safety of our animals for their entire lives. These animals rely on us to protect them for the duration of their lives, not ours.

My Story

My story as an animal lover, and an attorney for that matter, started when I was very young. I have always loved animals, and felt very deeply connected with them. Our family had the quintessential loving family dog and cat growing up, and I was also blessed to know several horses. Animals are always teaching us, if we let them, and I received the finest education from the animals I have been lucky enough to know in my life.

I can remember wanting to be an attorney from a very early age, but that all changed when I entered high school and studied biology. That's when I fell in love with science, and decided to change course to become either a marine biologist or an equine veterinarian. As I graduated high school and headed off to Cornell University, the thought of a life working with animals seemed like a dream come true.

But that was all destined to change again. My experience as a freshman in the Animal Science Department was not what I had anticipated. I came face-to-face with the realities of what being an Animal Science major meant, and it wasn't for me. Vivisection, testing, experimentation, and slaughter were all acts that went against my very being. I quickly moved on trying to figure out where to go next.

After trying a few different programs of study, I ended up in a Business Law class that immediately ignited my love of the law. After the very first class, I knew that I wanted to go to law school and become an attorney. I could feel in my heart that it was what I was meant to do. At the time I thought being an attorney meant giving up a career of working with animals, but I just wasn't seeing all of the possibilities.

The truth is that animals need attorneys more than you might realize. They are an interest without a voice, and they rely on humans to protect their welfare. If we neglect or fail at this task, it is all of us who suffer. I now realize that, as an attorney, I can contribute to protecting the welfare of animals in many ways, both large and small. One way is by helping other animal lovers understand the legal environment that animals face, and by providing them with tools to protect their own animals from the precarious uncertainty so many animals must struggle to endure.

The reality is that most animal lovers, through no fault of their own, are not aware of the information contained within these pages, and this has tragic consequences for their animals. My goal is to encourage animal lovers to educate themselves, and do some simple planning. It may present some inconvenience and expense to you, but it may be a matter of life and death for your animal. And if you are reading this, my guess is you would agree that these animals do not deserve a fate left to chance when there are steps we can take to guarantee them a safe future.

I believe the honor and responsibility of caring for an animal is one that lasts for that animal's entire life. When I adopt an animal, I become a steward of that animal's life, and it is up to me to make sure that animal is protected and cared for even if something happens to me. I believe that truly loving and caring for your animal means making sure your animal has a good life for its entire life. It's not difficult to achieve, it just takes a little bit of planning.

This book is written as a call-to-action for animal owners everywhere to do just that: plan for their animals. I did not want to write a typical legal book filled with a bunch of boring, albeit useful, information. Instead, I wanted to give you the "brass tacks" version of why planning for your animal is so crucial, and what you need to know to get it taken care of. I wouldn't waste your time.

I also want to iterate, as I will throughout the book, that finding an experienced attorney you trust and enjoy working with will be essential to the planning process. If you ever have any questions or need further guidance, you can always feel free to email me. My goal is to facilitate the planning process for animal owners as much as possible, and to keep those sweet souls, like Twink, out of shelters forever.

Where are the Forms & Filler?

You may or may not have noticed, but there are no forms included with this book. What I mean by that is there is no CD or website included with the book that contains samples of the types of documents I will be talking about. Let me explain why.

Unless you are an attorney, you should not be using these forms. This book is not written for attorneys, so there is no need for the forms. If I included them, you might be tempted to use them yourself, and that would most likely result in more harm than good.

This book is written for you, the animal lover. It is designed to give you the information you need to take the best action to protect your animal. Throughout this book, I will stress the importance of working with a qualified estate planning attorney that you actually like. That's the person you want drafting the documents discussed in this book, and they don't need the forms. They have their own.

You may also notice that there are not any extensive appendices at the end of the book, or what I call filler. You might expect to find lots of charts and tables, or excerpts of legal code from each State, but that's not really the information that you need. You need to know why it is so important to plan for your animal, and you need to be motivated to do it! You don't need the filler, your attorney does, and again, they already have it.

Time is precious for us all. I don't want to waste your time. If you are reading this, then I know you love your animal, and you just need to know what you can do to protect it. The good news is that the message is short and sweet. Animals, like Twink, who once had loving homes, end up in shelters, and sadly worse, every single day. Without a plan, your animal could be one of them faster than you think. Planning for your animal is essential if you want to guarantee your animal is protected for its entire life. This book tells you how to do it.

Quick Diversion to Cover Estate Planning Basics

Before we talk about the best way for you to protect your animal, it will be helpful to cover some estate planning basics.

What is estate planning?

It is the process of planning your affairs in the event of your incapacity or death. It's important stuff, and while most people are aware that they need to undertake at least some form of estate planning, they may not fully understand why.

Many of the reasons are the same regardless of whether you have animals or not. You want to make sure your affairs are handled the way you want in the event something happens to you. You also want to make sure you leave the right people in charge. You don't want to leave things to chance, and you don't want to waste money and time on things like probate and taxes.

More importantly, however, you want to make sure that your loved ones are taken care of. You want to alleviate as much stress as you possibly can for them. Experiencing your loss will be hard enough, so you want to take as many steps as you can to protect your loved ones and make things easier on them. This is really the "why" of estate planning. It's not only to protect ourselves, but really to protect those we love, including our animals.

So let's take a look at a few common estate planning approaches.

Intestate Succession - The Do-Nothing Approach

Intestate succession is what happens to your estate if you don't have any estate planning documents whatsoever, or what is commonly called the do-nothing approach. It is the absolute worst approach you can take, especially if you have children or animals.

If you do nothing, your estate will be probated and state law will determine who receives your estate. In some cases it could even be the state itself!

And don't just skip over that word probate; it is not to be ignored. Probate is the court-supervised process necessary to distribute someone's estate when they pass away either with or without a Will. In short, probate is considered cruel and unusual punishment by many people because it is super expensive and takes forever. Seriously, in California a really fast probate is 18 months, and it is not uncommon for the probate process to last anywhere from two to four years. Suffice it to say that the only people who are happy about probate are the attorneys, courts, and court officials who are all collecting huge fees. In California, someone with a gross estate (meaning they don't care how much debt you have) of $1 million will be paying about $45,000 in probate fees. If that sounds shocking, that's because it is. The do-nothing approach will cost you A LOT more than if you had done some basic planning. That's right, if you thought you were saving money by doing nothing, you thought wrong.

The do-nothing approach not only ends up being time-consuming and expensive, but also gives you zero control over who receives your property and zero control over who makes decisions for you. The court will decide all of this for you. You have no say, no control, and no power. To add insult to injury, the entire process is also a part of the public record for all to see, meaning there is no privacy for you or your family.

Another fatal flaw of the do-nothing approach is that it also leaves you completely vulnerable in the event of your incapacity. There will be no one to handle your affairs, no one to make medical decisions for you, and no opportunity to make your wishes known in critical situations. A guardianship or conservatorship may have to be established by a court, which is another expensive and time-consuming process.

Leaving your affairs to chance in the event of incapacity can have unimaginable consequences. This is particularly true when it comes to your medical decisions and your dependents. You may find yourself with doctors and treatments you never would have wanted because a court has decided who makes your medical decisions. The court and state law will also decide who raises your children and/or what happens to your animals.

The do-nothing approach can have disastrous consequences, and it is not an approach that anyone should take when it comes to planning their estate. Again, this is particularly true if you have children or animals.

Will-Based Planning - The Halfway Approach

A Will is a legal document that distributes the property left in your estate at your death. You have the option of giving specific items of property to specific people and/or organizations, and/or giving your entire estate to specific people and/or organizations. To be legally enforceable, a Will must satisfy numerous formalities and be properly executed. When you pass away, the person you have left in charge, otherwise known as your executor, has to petition the local court to probate your estate and distribute it according to the terms of your Will.

You should be aware that serving as executor is not the "honor" it may first appear to be, and "poor bastard" may be a more appropriate title for the job. This is the case for a couple of different reasons. First, and foremost, your executor has to *probate* your Will, and we just went over the fact that probate is considered cruel and unusual punishment by many people. Second, it is actually a big burden to be named someone's executor. There is a tremendous amount of work, stress, and time involved. Finally, the person serving as executor is often not compensated for their time and effort, nor are they likely to receive much thanks and appreciation.

I refer to the Will as the halfway-approach because it solves about half of the problems associated with intestate succession, a.k.a the do-nothing approach.

A Will does give you more control over who is the beneficiary of your estate, and you have the ability to appoint your decision makers. These are two big pluses, but unfortunately, there are still two overwhelming negatives. First, your estate still has to go through the lengthy, very expensive, and completely public process of probate, yuck! Second, a Will is also completely useless in the event of your incapacity, because it is only effective when you pass away. A comprehensive power of attorney will cover certain situations in the event of incapacity, but it is not nearly enough to protect your animals or your children. This is why a Will should be a part of your estate plan, but not the central component.

Another major drawback of a Will is that you are not allowed to put conditions on any of the property that you transfer. This is not only a huge inconvenience, but can also have disastrous consequences for humans and animals alike. Make a note of this, as we will discuss it further in just a few pages. Suffice it to say for now, that if you are planning to protect your animal a Will may actually create more problems than it solves.

Intestate succession and Will-based planning are generally not good options for anyone, even someone who does not own animals. There is just too much left to chance. Not to mention the unnecessary delays, expense, and disclosure of your personal affairs to the public-at-large that probate will require. For all of these reasons and more, the revocable living trust (RLT) has become the most ubiquitous estate planning tool.

Trust-Based Planning - A Complete Solution

The revocable living trust (RLT) allows a person to privately and seamlessly transfer the management of their affairs to another person in the event of their incapacity or death. The RLT avoids probate, and is not subject to the same limits or restrictions on property transfers as a Will. This makes RLTs very appealing and commonly used estate planning tools. This type of estate planning is called trust-based planning, and it is the preferred planning approach for anyone who has animals.

The basic RLT works like this. You, the grantor (another name for the person creating the original trust), create the RLT and transfer your property into the trust. You also designate successor or back-up trustees to manage the trust, and beneficiaries to receive and/or benefit from the trust property. While you are alive, the RLT is like your alter-ego. You serve as trustee, and you enjoy complete use and enjoyment of your property. You can also amend or terminate the trust any time you wish during your life, and upon your passing, your trust will become irrevocable (meaning it can't be changed or amended). In the event of your incapacity or death, your successor trustee will take-over and manage your trust and trust property pursuant to the language of your RLT.

It is important to select at least two to three backup trustees. Again, because you never know what the future holds, and it is always a good idea to have backups.

Many people have a hard time deciding who to appoint as their successor trustee, and aren't exactly sure what characteristics this person should have. A good trustee is someone who is honest, organized, accountable, and a good communicator. It is also a good idea to name successor trustees that are younger than you, for soberingly obvious reasons.

All trustees have a fiduciary duty to administer the trust according to the trust document and for the benefit of the beneficiaries. Basically, this means that they are legally obligated to follow the trust document, and act in the best interests of the trust and the trust beneficiaries. As trustee, you cannot put your own interests first. Thus, honesty and integrity are two of the most essential characteristics of a trustee.

A comprehensive trust-based estate planning portfolio will not only include one or more RLTs, but also your pour-over Will, your durable power of attorney, your health care documents, as well as several ancillary documents.

Your pour-over Will is a Will that acts as a safety net, and works in tandem with your RLT. In most cases when you set-up your RLT, you transfer all of your property to the RLT. This process is called "funding" the trust, and it is this process that allows you to fully realize the benefits of your trust. It doesn't do any good to create a RLT if you don't put your property inside of it.

If a piece of property is not inside the trust, then it "falls" outside the trust and is "caught" by your pour-over Will which "pours" that piece of property back into your RLT. Any property "caught" by your pour-over Will would still need to be probated, which is why the pour-over Will is referred to as a "safety net". It avoids many of the unwanted consequences of the do-nothing approach, and ensures your property is distributed according to the terms of your trust. Ideally, however, all of your property is inside your trust, your pour-over Will is never needed, and your estate avoids probate completely.

Your durable power of attorney authorizes your "agent" (someone you designate) to manage your affairs in the event of your incapacity. It is extremely important that your power of attorney be comprehensive and properly drafted. Otherwise, your agent may not have the authority and/or powers they need to manage your affairs. Third parties may also refuse to honor the power of attorney or transact business with your agents.

Given the increasingly litigious nature of society, many third parties are reluctant to rely on a power of attorney that simply grants the agent broad, sweeping powers. Instead, they prefer a comprehensive power of attorney that not only includes language granting the agent broad, sweeping powers, but also specifically identifies and describes in detail many of the powers that your agent holds. This gives third parties relying on the power of attorney the comfort they need to transact business with your agents.

Your health care documents consist of your privacy waivers, your health care power of attorney, and possibly, your living will. These documents authorize doctors to release information about your medical condition, and they identify who is to make medical decisions on your behalf. A living will is a statement of your desire for your life to not be artificially prolonged under certain circumstances. Again, it is absolutely crucial that these health care documents are properly drafted. Hospitals and doctors are very careful to avoid liability, and your documents must meet all of the necessary legal requirements. Otherwise, doctors and hospitals will not honor them.

I always encourage people to start the estate planning process earlier rather than later, and the ones that do have the best end results. This is not to say that once you do it, you are done forever. Your estate planning documents are living, breathing documents, and they need to be updated to stay current with you and the world we live in.

If you have never done any estate planning, now is the time! Get out there, find an attorney you like, and get it done. It will feel good to have it taken care of, and you will be doing yourself and everyone who loves you a huge favor.

P.S. It will be a bit expensive, but not as expensive as the alternative. You need to think of the estate planning process as an investment in yourself, your family, and your estate. Always remember, it is less expensive to have a comprehensive estate plan in place than it is to do nothing. If you do nothing, the best case scenario, if you can call it that, is that you are not alive and you never know how much of your estate was wasted on probate fees, professional fees, filing fees, taxes, and possibly even litigation. It will be your loved ones that are stuck holding the proverbial "check."

Estate planning is not an area where you want to try and cut corners to save money. You will pay for it down the line and it's not worth it.

Animals as Property & the Problem with Wills

A root cause of many of the problems facing animals in today's world is that all animals are treated as "property" under the law. For purposes of estate planning, this means animals are treated no differently from other items of your property such as your clothing, furniture, books, etc. At first glance, this may seem like no big deal. But after reading this section, you will begin to understand why the fact that animals are treated as property can have tragic, unintended consequences for the animals in our lives. You will also see why Wills cannot adequately protect your animal.

First, a Will is only effective upon your death, and if you are incapacitated, someone needs to be authorized to care for your animal. Animals are very sensitive, and they often know when something is wrong with someone they love. Many vets will tell you that it is not uncommon for an animal to experience various stress and depression related conditions when something has happened to its owner. They will also tell you that providing care for an animal when the owner is absent may not be something they are willing to do, because doing so might expose them to liability. That is, of course, unless the proper planning has been done.

Without the proper planning, a veterinarian can find themselves in a tricky legal spot if an animal requires medical attention and the owner is incapacitated. Before they can perform services on the animal, they need to know that the owner authorizes the services, and that the services will be paid for. Otherwise, the veterinarian may be faced with a lawsuit from the animal's owner, and be out-of-pocket for the costs of the services. Thus, most veterinarians will refuse to provide services without the owner's consent.

Again, this can have disastrous consequences for your animal. If you are incapacitated, by definition you are not physically and/or mentally able to authorize veterinary services for your animal. If you're dead you certainly can't give your authorization, and if your estate is left in limbo, it may be months before your representatives can give such authorization. This is something that you need to plan for in advance. A well-meaning friend who will take care of your animal is not enough. If your animal requires a vet's attention, your friend needs to be able to prove that she is legally authorized to care for your animal. She will also need to show her ability to pay for the vet's services.

Another major drawback of a Will is that your Will must be properly executed and satisfy numerous legal formalities, otherwise, it will be invalid. Some of these formalities are rooted in centuries of legal opinions, while others are subject to change at any point in time. The pressing point is that if your Will does not conform to these required formalities, your Will is disregarded and your property passes according to your state's intestate succession laws. Basically, it's as though you took the "do-nothing" approach.

Unfortunately, with the advent of do-it-yourself online legal solutions, many people are tempted to save money and take the estate planning process into their own hands. This is a terrible idea, and one that should be avoided at all costs. When it comes to your estate, your loved ones, and your animals, there is too much on the line to take shortcuts. These shortcuts will end up costing a lot of time and money at some point down the line, and could even cost your animal its life.

When it comes to any kind of estate planning, the best solution is to find an attorney you trust, who can guide you through the process, and ensure that you are executing valid documents that meet all of the formalities required by your state. Otherwise, you're being "penny-wise and pound-foolish" as the saying goes.

Another major pitfall of using a Will when planning for an animal is our old friend: probate. If you have animals, it is <u>essential</u> for you to avoid probate. First, animals don't have time for the probate process. If you pass away, they need care immediately. In California, a very basic probate will last anywhere from 18-24 months, possibly leaving your animal in an extremely dangerous limbo. During this time it may be very unclear who should take possession of and care for your animal. It may also be very difficult to use any of the estate monies to pay for any of your animal's basic care. This is clearly not a good situation for your animal.

If you're still thinking about relying on a Will to leave your animal to someone, this next fact should get that thought out of your head once and for all. When someone is left property in a Will, that person can do whatever they want with the property. When it comes to your animal that means the person can literally do whatever they want with your animal. This would include giving it away to another person, having it euthanized, surrendering it to a shelter, or even selling it for commercial purposes or experimentation. There is absolutely nothing to stop this from happening.

For example, I once knew of a woman with a Will who left all of her property to her daughter. The property in the woman's estate included a horse, and the daughter did not want the horse. So, she decided that a quick and easy way to turn the horse into some money would be to sell it for horsemeat. This particular horse was lucky enough to be rescued from its holding pen before being shipped over the border to Mexico, but others are not so lucky. Many animals that are left to someone in a Will end up in shelters, or worse.

Some individuals try to solve this problem by including conditions on the transfer in the language of their Will. For example, "I give my cat, Fluffy, to Linda as long as Linda keeps Fluffy forever, feeds her every day, and never lets her outside." However, the only part of the above sentence that has any legal meaning in a Will is the part that says "I give my cat, Fluffy, to Linda", the rest is meaningless and is not legally binding in any way whatsoever. You cannot put conditions on property that you leave to someone in your Will. The reasoning for this is rooted in the idea that it is bad to restrict the use and alienability of property, particularly real property. However, this reasoning extends to all types of property, including your animals.

Now it should be clear why relying on a Will can have disastrous consequences for animals and their owners.

Planning for your animal can truly be a matter of life and death for your animal. The "do-nothing" approach is the worst thing you can do. It is the equivalent of rolling the dice and leaving your animal's life to chance. Relying on a Will isn't much better. If our goal is to protect our animals for the duration of *their* lives, not ours, then we need a more comprehensive solution. The good news is that one exists.

It comes in the form of a revocable living trust (RLT) that is modified to include your animal. RLTs are the preferred estate planning tool for a reason, and you may already have one in place that can be easily amended to add provisions to protect your animal. If you don't, then this should be another great reason to get your estate planning taken care of immediately. The RLT not only protects you and your loved ones while preserving your estate, but also provides an effective solution for protecting your animal.

The Animal Care Trust: An Ideal Solution for Animal Owners

Now we will take a closer look at the ideal solution for anyone who wants a simple plan to protect their beloved animal. Please keep in mind that everyone's situation is different, and for purposes of the conversation here, I will be speaking very generally. Again, it is essential for you to meet with your personal planning attorney so that this general solution may be customized to your specific situation and needs.

Since we have already outlined some of the many benefits of trust-based planning, it should come as no surprise that a RLT will be the preferred vehicle when it comes to planning for your animal. This is how it works.

The Animal Care Trust

The primary component of your overall plan to protect your animal is either a separate, standalone RLT dedicated as an Animal Care Trust (ACT) or provisions within your existing RLT for an ACT. For purposes of our discussion here the distinction between the two is irrelevant. Suffice it to say that if you have a very simple, straightforward situation you will probably be looking at the latter. If your situation is more complex and nuanced, then you will probably need the former. Either way, if you already have an RLT in place, you are one step ahead of the game. If you don't, well there's no time like the present to get it done.

Think of your ACT as the suitcase that holds everything you need to protect your animal. It keeps everything in one place and working together. The ACT contains all of the essential language and provisions necessary to protect your animal. It identifies your back-up trustees and caretakers, and contains the instructions they are required to follow. It also holds all trust property, including your animal and all monies necessary to care for your animal.

When creating your ACT, it will be necessary for you to put some thought into who you should appoint as your successor trustees and caretakers. It is very important that you choose wisely in this regard. You will also need to think about the instructions that you want to provide your trustee and caretaker. These instructions not only include the requirements for caring for your animal, but also provide critical guidelines and rules for your trustee and caretaker to follow. If these rules are not followed there may be consequences for either the caretaker or the trustee. Hopefully, this type of enforcement is never necessary, and one sure way to avoid it is by carefully selecting your trustee.

The Trustee

You will be the initial trustee of the ACT, and you will appoint two to three back-up trustees to take over in case something happens to you. Deciding who will be your successor, a.k.a. back-up, trustees is a very important decision. An ideal trustee is someone who likes animals, is a good communicator, and is an organized person of the highest moral character.

Your trustee is going to be serving a very important role and holds a lot of power, so be sure you choose these individuals with prudence. When planning for an animal, it is best to name a trustee that does not serve any other roles. Ideally, the trustee should not be the caretaker, a beneficiary, or any other party. Otherwise, conflicts of interest can occur and our system of checks and balances falls apart.

For example, many people wonder if the back-up trustee is the same person that will serve as your animal's caretaker. The answer is absolutely not. This is because your trustee is responsible for overseeing the caretaker, which is an important check in a system of checks and balances designed to protect your animal no matter what the future holds. In fact, your trustee does not necessarily have to be a big "animal person", although it is certainly better if they at least like animals. It is difficult for a trustee to properly administer a trust designed to protect your animal if they do not even like them. More importantly, can you trust someone that doesn't like animals?

One final note on trustee selection: it is possible to appoint more than one trustee at a time. Meaning, there would be multiple trustees, or co-trustees, serving. If this is an appealing option to you, it is crucial that you have a dispute resolution mechanism in place to resolve disagreements between your trustees. Otherwise, the trustees may find themselves wasting a lot of time and money, or even worse, in an expensive court battle fighting over which trustee is right.

Trustee Instructions

Now that you've created the ACT and selected your successor trustees, the next step is to tell them what to do.

The trustee of the ACT will serve two primary roles: they will be responsible for overseeing and distributing any monies that are required for your animal's care; and they will be responsible for checking in to make sure that your animal's caretaker is taking proper care of your animal. Thus, your instructions to the trustee will let them know when it is appropriate to directly pay for your animal's expenses and/or when to give money to your animal's caretaker. Your instructions will also tell your trustee how often they should check in on your animal, what to look for to be sure the caretaker is providing the proper care, and what to do in the event they are not.

For example, if your caretaker is not following the animal care instructions contained within the ACT, then the trustee may be instructed to remove the caretaker and appoint the next back-up caretaker. This is a very important enforcement mechanism, and just knowing it exists can dramatically shape people's attitudes and actions. It's a powerful indicator that caring for your animal is serious business, which of course it is. We have already seen that it can be a matter of life or death. This is why the ACT is so important, it puts everything together in a legally enforceable package to guarantee that your animal is protected, leaving nothing to chance.

If all goes well, the caretaker provides a loving, caring home for your animal for the rest of its life. All expenses are paid for by the trustee out of trust monies, and anything left over is distributed to your final beneficiaries. Of course, your trust will also include language to handle situations where things go wrong. If you're ready for it, then it's less likely to happen, and there's no harm in planning for worse-case-scenarios when it comes to planning for your animal. The most common problems are problems with the caretaker, so needless to say, it is vital that you choose wisely in this regard. Arguably, the most important component in your plan to protect your animal is your caretaker.

Animal Caretaker

Being a huge animal lover may not be the number one criteria when selecting your trustee, but it most certainly is when selecting your animal's caretaker. The caretaker is the person entrusted to provide your animal with the love, care, and attention they deserve. This person needs to truly love and understand animals. They need to either have animals of their own, or at least have experience taking care of them.

It is never a good idea to appoint a caretaker that has never cared for an animal before. Someone may have the best of intentions, but may not fully appreciate the amount of time, attention, and money that is needed to properly care for an animal. However, if this is your only option, you must take additional steps to make sure any novice caretakers are well-vetted. The goal is to be certain you have found someone who is comfortable with the practical realities of caring for your animal.

It is also ideal if your animal's caretaker is someone that already has a relationship with your animal, and is someone your animal is accustomed to seeing and visiting with. This will make the transition to a life without you a little bit easier for your animal. If your animal's caretaker is someone your animal has never met before, it's certainly not the end of the world. Animals have an amazing ability to adapt, and they adjust to life changes better than we can imagine. The most important characteristic of a quality caretaker is that they unconditionally love your animal, and will provide it with the very best of care.

For all intents and purposes, your animal's caretaker will become your animal's new family. They will not legally own your animal, but they will be responsible for its day-to-day care. It is important that you carefully select someone who loves your animal, and is excited about making them a part of their family if/when that time comes. Also, while your caretaker may not have the opportunity to have a pre-existing relationship with your animal, it is absolutely critical that you make your caretaker aware of your plans before you execute your planning documents. It should NEVER be a surprise to your caretaker that they have been selected to care for your animal. Surprises like this are a recipe for disaster.

It is also a good idea to name at least two to three back-up caretakers for your animal. This way, if something happens to your first caretaker, your animal will have another loving home all lined up. It is also a good idea to select an organization of last resort, just in case you run-out of backup caretakers. This should be a no-kill animal rescue organization that will carefully place your animal in a loving home. The idea here is that it is better to name an organization of last resort, rather than leave your animal's life to chance. Otherwise, you have no ability to control where your animal ends up if something happens to your caretakers.

It is always prudent to contact your preferred organization of last resort to let them know of your desired plans. You will want to verify that the rescue organization of last resort will agree to take your animal if/when the time comes. You may also need to make financial arrangements for the organization to accept your animal. As animal owners, we are very aware that animals come with expenses, and it is important to keep this in mind when selecting caretakers and your organization of last resort.

Finally, it is important that you never name joint caretakers, meaning two caretakers who are serving at the same time. This is another recipe for disaster, and opens the door to battles between the caretakers. It is fine to establish a team of people who will assist your caretaker, for example, you may wish to list groomers, sitters, vets, and other professionals that may help care for your animal. Just don't give more than one person the actual title and position of caretaker.

It is always fine to name back-up caretakers, you just don't want two serving at the same time. It's the same reasoning when it comes to naming guardians for children. You don't want to name two people, because you may be unintentionally setting the stage for a custody battle. Remember, you don't have a crystal ball, so you need to plan accordingly.

Caretakers are a vital part of your plan to protect your animal. It is essential that you carefully select these individuals, make them aware of your plans, and discuss the practical realities of caring for your animal with them. You want to ensure that they are comfortable with taking on this role, and that you are doing everything you can to set them up for success This will include providing your caretaker with the necessary instructions.

Animal Care Instructions

Now that you've decided who will be your animal's caretaker, you will need to provide them with the information they need to properly care for your animal. Depending on your particular situation, this section of your overall plan to protect your animal may be as simple as a few sentences, or as comprehensive as you desire. The main purpose of the animal care instructions is to establish the minimum standards of care that your animal's caretaker must provide. Beyond that, these instructions serve as a guide to help your caretaker take the best possible care of your animal.

This would be an example of the simplest of situations. Olive is a single person with a dog named Duke. Olive names Cary, a close friend and fellow dog lover, as Duke's caretaker in the event that something happens to Olive. Cary has dogs of her own that play with Duke several times a week, and Cary has taken care of Duke on several occasions when Olive has been out-of-town. Olive is 100% confident in Cary's ability to love and care for Duke, and thus, she is comfortable leaving the details of Duke's care to Cary's discretion. The instructions for Duke's care will include the basics that are necessary, leaving the rest in Cary's capable hands.

In this situation, it is very likely that Duke will spend the remainder of his days in Cary's loving home. However, there is the possibility that something could happen to Cary. This is where it becomes important to name back-up caretakers for Duke, and include a more comprehensive set of instructions for Duke's care. An extensive and detailed set of instructions will be extremely useful to a caretaker who does not know Duke as well. Remember, it is always a good idea to have a few back-up plans.

A more complicated example would be a situation where Olive owns five horses, ranging in age and special needs. Each horse may have its own set of caretakers and care instructions. In addition, Olive may decide to establish a team of professionals that will be available to assist with the horses' care including equine veterinarians, farriers, trainers, etc. In this case the care instructions may be quite substantial and more complex. The more complicated and obscure your animal's care may be, the greater the need for a comprehensive set of animal care instructions.

Your animal care instructions are your opportunity to provide your caretaker with the details and finer points of your animal's care. Include the basics, but also include the little things that make life just a little bit better for your animal. Remember, your animal will miss you, so do everything you can to ensure it is comforted by a familiar routine and environment.

Keeping the Animals at Home

A question that often arises is "Can my animal stay in my house for the rest of its life?" The answer is a resounding "yes". Many animal owners feel very strongly that they do not want their beloved animal to be uprooted to another home. Instead, they are willing to make their home available as a residence to the caretaker so that their animal may continue life there with as little interruption as possible.

While this may not be feasible or desirable for every animal owner, if you do want your animal to remain in your home, rest assured that this is completely possible. Your planning documents will simply have to include additional provisions to address the issues of continued home ownership, maintenance, and the rights and responsibilities of the caretaker as a resident. Additional financial analysis and planning may also have to be undertaken to account for any additional costs.

There will be an additional layer of complexity and expense if your desire is to keep your animal living in your house. However, if it's an option for you, it is well worth it. This is especially true if you have a situation involving an animal that would not do well outside of its familiar home environment or you have multiple animals.

For example, the concept of "the pack" is extremely important to dogs, and all you need is two or more dogs to make a pack. Imagine a situation where a couple has a pack of four dogs. If at all possible, they want to make sure their dogs stay together, and they want them to stay in their home. So, they create a plan for their dogs.

The plan names the dogs' groomer as the initial caregiver, and names their dog-sitter as the back-up. The caregiver is required to live in their home and take care of the dogs until the last dog passes away. When the final dog passes, the house is sold and all remaining trust property is distributed to their beneficiaries. They make their caretakers aware of their plans, address any concerns their caretakers have, and leave them the necessary instructions. They also appoint a trustee to implement the ACT, oversee the caretaker, and otherwise administer the terms of their RLT.

The home can be just as important to animals as it is to us, and preserving your home for your animal's continued use can be a wonderful option in many situations.

The Money

There is no getting around the fact that finances are a major part of making all of this work. It is unrealistic to expect someone to care for your animal without at least covering the animal's expenses. Thus, in addition to legally owning your animal, your ACT will also own the assets and/or accounts needed to cover the costs of your animal's care. At a minimum these costs will include food, bedding, grooming, and veterinary care. Depending on your situation, these expenses can be quite substantial. The trustee of the ACT will be responsible for managing the assets and/or accounts owned by the trust, and for disbursing monies to pay for the costs of your animal's care.

You should also consider the question of whether or not you should compensate your animal's caretaker. The answer depends on the situation, but it is usually a wise thing to do. It is always a blessing to be on the receiving end of someone's kindness, but it is not something you should expect or rely upon. The bottom line is that the caretaker is taking on an additional responsibility, and the best way to show that you value that undertaking is by compensating your caretaker. It is a gesture that will go a long way to ensure the quality of life for your animal.

For example, in the case of Olive, Duke, and Cary, the ACT should provide monies to cover the costs of Duke's care as well as nominal compensation for Cary. This will help ensure that Cary does not feel taken advantage of. Cary may never feel this way, but unfortunately, we cannot predict her future feelings, and this is an easy way to ensure this does not become an issue.

Some owners are concerned that compensating the caretaker could create a situation where the caretaker is receiving compensation, but is not really caring for the animal. Fortunately, this would be a situation where the trustee of the ACT would have the power to remove and replace the caregiver, and in doing so, the compensation would cease as well.

If you are concerned that the value of your assets may not be sufficient to cover the costs of your animal's care, then you may want to consider a life insurance policy that will provide the necessary funding at the time of your death. If compensating your caretaker is simply not something you can afford, then it is vital to select a caretaker who is aware of this, and who is willing to accept financial responsibility for your animal.

However, be aware that it may be very difficult to enforce any of the caretaker instructions if the caretaker is not receiving any compensation. It will be even more difficult if the caretaker is going out-of-pocket, without reimbursement, to cover the costs of caring for your animal. This is because for a contract to be legally binding both parties have to receive something, it's called a bargained-for exchange, or consideration. Without it, the contract is unenforceable. This is another reason why even nominally compensating your caretaker is advised.

Oversight & Enforcement

To truly appreciate the protection your ACT will provide your animal, it is necessary to understand how the ACT is enforced. The ability to enforce your plan must be built-in to the structure of your plan. Otherwise, your plan is nothing more than hopes and wishes, not the legally enforceable, guaranteed protection that your animal needs. It is the ACT's ability to be enforced that truly protects your animal. None of us have a crystal ball, and the checks and balances of an ACT are necessary to guarantee your animal is protected for its entire life, no matter what the future holds.

This is true even when you have a perfect caregiver that for all practical purposes requires no supervision or oversight. In this situation many owners are tempted to leave their animal to someone with a lump-sum of money because they have 100% faith in their caregiver. However, this is a terrible strategy for a couple of reasons.

First, it does not protect your animal if something happens to the caregiver. If the caretaker dies without an ACT in place, then your animal may find itself surrendered to a shelter. With an ACT, there is a trustee who will not only know if anything happens to your caretaker, but can also guarantee your animal is placed with the next caretaker and never in a shelter.

Second, unfortunately it is impossible to predict someone's future behavior. Even the seemingly perfect caregiver can end up being someone who doesn't work out. Furthermore, it may be impossible to predict the circumstances causing such an outcome. The ACT is the mechanism that protects your animal regardless of what the future holds for the caretaker.

The trustee of your ACT will be responsible for overseeing your animal's caretaker, and ensuring that the terms of your ACT are being adhered to. If the caretaker is not providing the required level of care and/or there are other grounds for removal, the trustee will have the power to remove and replace the caretaker with the next successor caretaker. The trustee's ability to remove and replace the caretaker is one of the most essential enforcement mechanisms of the ACT.

The trustee's ability to oversee the monies used to care for your animal is another important safeguard. It prevents the caretaker from abusing or misappropriating any of the monies you have set aside for the care of your animal. A well-designed system of checks and balances that includes enforcement mechanisms will guarantee that your animal is receiving the care you expect.

In some cases, the selection of your animal's caretakers and your animal care instructions will manifest themselves in the form of a contract with the caretaker, referred to as an Animal Caretaker Agreement (ACA). The ACA is a legally binding contract that obligates your caretaker to care for your animal pursuant to the instructions contained within the ACA. This means that your caretaker cannot deviate from the ACA without consequences. If the caretaker violates the ACA, they can be removed as caretaker and replaced by the next back-up caretaker.

It is impossible to predict the future, so it is important to include failsafe mechanisms that can be triggered to ensure your animal is being cared for according to your wishes. The ACA will provide an added layer of protection for your animal, and again, it conveys the message to your caretaker that caring for your animal is serious business. ACAs are useful in many cases, and are strongly advised if you will be appointing a professional caretaker.

Trust Protectors

The trustee's oversight over the caretaker is an important part of the system of checks and balances contained within the ACT. However, it is also important to have a failsafe mechanism in place to ensure the trustee does not abuse their powers. This mechanism is the trust protector.

Trustee abuse is always a concern, and drafting your plan to prevent and mitigate such abuse is important regardless of whether you have animals. Use of a trust protector will prevent trustee abuse and waste, and it will keep everyone out of court. Remember going to court means a huge waste of time and money, and it puts your animal in a dangerous limbo. A trust protector avoids this by vesting someone with the power to remove and replace a trustee that is not fulfilling their obligations. The trust protector may also be given other special powers to further protect your estate, your animals, and your beneficiaries.

Without a trust protector, your beneficiaries will be forced to file an expensive lawsuit if they want to remove a trustee who is abusing their power. The trustee will of course defend themselves in the lawsuit, and may exhaust the trust assets to fund their defense. That's a terrible situation for your beneficiaries to find themselves in, not to mention your animal. The use of a trust protector will avoid this by giving the trust protector the powers to do what is necessary to enforce the terms of the ACT. The trust protector is given powers that no one else will hold, and it is important to select the right person to serve as trust protector.

A trust protector should never be someone that is named elsewhere in the trust. You should not name your trustees, beneficiaries, caretakers, or any other party named in the trust as the trust protector. Also, the trust protector must not be related to or subordinate to any of the individuals named elsewhere in the trust. You want to name someone who will serve in this role, and only this role, if the time comes. Ideally, it never does and the trust protector is just another back-up plan that you never need. In the event it does become necessary for your trust protector to take action, it's important that you have entrusted this position to someone who is intelligent, responsible, and of the highest moral character. Attorneys, CPAs, and other trusted advisors are often a wise choice.

Putting it All Together

Here's a simple example of how everything works together in our hypothetical with Olive and Duke.

Please note the part in the following scenario where emergency responders are able to find Olive's emergency contact information in the glove compartment of her car. This is incredibly important. Make it easy for emergency responders to find medical documents and emergency contact information. It is a very simple thing to do, and, as you will see below, it can make a real difference for you, your loved ones, and your animals.

Let's take a look at how everything works together using a hypothetical situation with some fictional characters.

Olive executes a comprehensive estate plan that includes an RLT with ACT provisions. Theresa, a close friend who loves animals and works as a financial advisor is named as successor trustee, along with two additional successor trustees to serve consecutively. Cary is selected as the animal caretaker, and signs an ACA. Two additional animal caretakers are named as back-ups.

All of Olive's property is transferred to the ACT, including Olive's dog, Duke. Other property transferred to the ACT includes Olive's primary residence, vehicles, bank accounts, and investment portfolios.

Everything is business as usual, until one day Olive is involved in a serious car accident. Fortunately, Olive had the foresight to include emergency contact information for Theresa and Cary, as well as copies of her health care documents, in the glove compartment of her car. The emergency responders contact Theresa and Cary and let them know the situation with Olive. Cary arrives at Olive's house within a few hours to take care of Duke, and Duke's care continues uninterrupted as a result of Olive's thoughtful planning.

Olive is hospitalized and in a coma. Given Olive's incapacity, Theresa is now serving as trustee of Olive's trust, and is managing the trust and its property pursuant to Olive's trust document. Cary is serving as Duke's caretaker and providing for Duke's care pursuant to the ACA.

A week later, Olive passes away as a result of injuries from the accident. As trustee, Theresa supervises the sale of Olive's home, and the monies from the sale are added to the trust. All of the trust monies are consolidated into a single bank account and an investment account. A portion of the monies are set aside in the bank account for any immediate expenses, and the rest are transferred to the investment account to be responsibly invested. Cary continues to take care of Duke, and Duke is very happy in his new home.

Pursuant to the ACA and the ACT, Theresa disburses trust funds as necessary to cover Duke's expenses and Cary's compensation as caretaker. Also pursuant to the ACT, Theresa checks in on Duke periodically and stays in regular contact with Cary. Thanks to Olive's careful planning, Duke's care has continued uninterrupted; saving Duke from a tremendous amount of additional stress and heartache.

In a perfect world, Duke lives out his days with Cary. When Duke dies, Theresa, as trustee, winds up the ACT and distributes the remaining ACT property to Olive's beneficiaries. In this case, Olive has named a local dog rescue as the beneficiary of the ACT, and they are extremely happy to get a donation.

Let's also take a look at what happens in a not-so-perfect world. These hypotheticals will demonstrate how the ACT and ACA work together when various issues arise.

Hypothetical No. 1

During Olive's hospitalization, Duke stops eating for several days. Cary decides it is necessary to take Duke to the veterinarian. She arrives for her appointment and shows her identification along with a copy of the ACA. Olive also had the foresight to put her vet on notice that Duke has back-up caretakers, so the ACA is already in Duke's file. Duke gets the treatment he needs and the trustee is billed for the services.

Many vets require payment at the time of service, so it is important that your animal's caretaker have the ability to pay for services, particularly in the case of an emergency. There are many ways to accomplish this. One is for the caretaker to pay for the expense out-of-pocket, and the trustee reimburses them using trust funds. This may work for small expenses, but it is not a good idea to rely on this option in the case of a true emergency where substantial funds may be needed.

A better option is to give your caretaker a credit/debit card that is tied to a trust bank account. It should be a special account that holds an emergency fund, rather than being the main trust account. Your trustee can add funds to it as they are depleted by your caretaker. This is a nice approach because your caretaker doesn't have to go out of pocket, and it doesn't give your caretaker access to all of the trust funds.

Hypothetical No. 2

Olive has passed away and Duke has been in Cary's care for a couple of years. Theresa, as trustee, notices that the frequency of veterinary expenses for Duke has dramatically increased. Theresa reaches out to Cary to find out what's going on. Cary says that Duke is fine, and that the veterinarian is running tests for preventative treatments. Theresa decides to contact the veterinarian directly to confirm this. As it turns out, Cary has been bringing her dogs in for veterinary services and using funds from Duke's ACT to pay for the services.

Theresa decides to discuss the problem with Cary directly. Cary is very embarrassed, and explains that she is having financial difficulties because she lost her job. Cary apologizes profusely, agrees to pay back the money, and promises it will never happen again. Theresa is in a difficult position, and wishes that Cary had not disclosed this information after the fact.

What should Theresa, as trustee, do next? Cary has not only misused trust funds, but also lied about it by not telling Theresa until afterwards. This makes the situation much worse. The language of Olive's ACT and ACA will control what happens in this situation, and there are a few different options depending on what Olive is most comfortable with.

If Olive has a zero-tolerance policy on this type of behavior, which would be entirely understandable, then the language of the ACT needs to clearly state that this is grounds for removing and replacing Duke's caretaker. Theresa would contact the next back-up caretaker for Duke, and make the necessary arrangements for Duke to be transferred to his new home. Cary would be notified and required to facilitate the transfer. The ACT and ACA would also need to include stiff penalties if Cary refuses to transfer possession of Duke. This would also be a crime since Duke does not legally belong to Cary.

Another option would be some type of "once a mistake, twice a fool" policy. Meaning, the ACT requires Cary to be put on probation, and if there is another violation of the ACT and/or ACA, then Cary is removed and replaced as caretaker.

A final option would be to leave the removal and replacement of the caretaker to the discretion of the trustee when the ACT or ACA has been violated. Obviously, this gives a lot of discretionary power to your trustee, so it is generally wise to include at least some guidelines for your trustee to follow.

There is also the option of a hybrid approach where there is mandatory removal for certain violations, probation and then removal for other types of violations, and some violations where removal is left to trustee discretion. As you can see this can all be highly customized to best suit the nuances of your particular situation. What's most important is enforceability in the real-world. That is what truly protects your animal. Putting together the ACT, naming trustees and caretakers, and assembling comprehensive instructions are all meaningless if nothing can be enforced in any practical way.

This is why it is truly important for you to sit down with an attorney that you not only trust, but who also fully understands contracts and estate planning. I continually stress the need to find an experienced attorney that you like because this is highly personal subject matter, and you need to feel extremely comfortable with the attorney you are sharing this information with. Your attorney really needs to understand the particulars of your situation to make sure everything is properly drafted, and most importantly, enforceable if the need arises. If you are looking at a situation where these agreements need to be enforced, you do not want to be relying on anything less than documents drafted by an experienced attorney who really understands what you need.

Hypothetical No. 3

Olive has passed away and Duke has been in Cary's care for a couple of years. Theresa has been acting as trustee, and overseeing the administration of the ACT. Unfortunately, one day Duke is hit by a car that veers off of the road. Cary is uninjured and quickly rushes Duke to the emergency vet hospital, where she authorizes whatever charges are necessary to save Duke's life.

Thankfully, the vets are able to rush Duke into surgery, saving his life, but Duke will need several weeks of rehabilitation at the vet hospital, before he is ready to come home.

Cary contacts Theresa to make her aware of the situation and to make arrangements for payment of the vet's bill, which is totaling about $15,000. Theresa informs Cary that the trust will not pay the bill, and that Cary should not have authorized the charges necessary to save Duke's life. The conversation does not end well, and Cary is worried that Duke will not be able to come home if the bill is not paid.

Cary has a copy of the ACT, and she decides to see if it gives her any guidance. The ACT states that Olive's estate attorney, AJ, has the power to appoint a trust protector to direct the trustee to follow the terms of the ACT. Cary contacts AJ and explains the situation. After following the procedures laid out in the ACT, AJ appoints a trust protector.

The trust protector reviews the trust, and it clearly states that the trustee must use trust funds to pay for Duke's medical care without limitation. The trust protector directs Theresa to pay the vet bill. If Theresa continues to refuse, the trust protector will remove Theresa as trustee and replace her with the next successor trustee.

This situation not only demonstrates how the trust protector oversees the trustee, it also shows how important it is to clearly define what you want. In this case, Olive made it clear that trust funds were to be used to save Duke no matter what. For many reasons, some people might prefer to set a limitation on this, so as not to completely exhaust the trust. For example, your ACT might state that trust funds may be used to pay for your animal's medical expenses up to $25,000 or another defined amount. The point is that it is better if you think things like this through, and if you decide what's best for your particular situation. This way, your wishes are clearly stated and your successors are not put in the position of trying to figure out what you would have wanted.

This example also demonstrates that it can be a very good idea to have insurance for your animal if you want your animal to receive the treatment it needs to save its life. Animal health care is becoming more and more expensive, and it is a tough decision to choose euthanasia because of financial limitations. Insurance can help you avoid this, and there are all different kinds of policies available. You have to do what is right for you and your animal, so research your options and see what works best for you.

If you are ever faced with the incredibly tough decision of having to euthanize your animal, this is something that I hope will give you some solace. You gave that animal a loving home until the end of its life. You know what happened to them. You were able to give them a safe and happy forever home. When you came into that animal's life you made sure your animal never again had to worry about facing the world alone, enduring the crushing experience of a life at a shelter, being labeled as unwanted, or worse.

There is a lot to be said for that.

Additional Considerations

Short Lived Animals

Many animals have average lifespans much shorter than our own, and when planning for your animal, this is actually a good thing. It is much easier to plan for an animal that will live 10-20 years versus an animal that could live for over a hundred years. This is because you want to name caretakers that you expect to outlive your animal, and this will be easier to do if your animal has a life span on the shorter side.

Good planning is all about setting things up for success, and ideally, you don't want your animals to have to move from caretaker to caretaker. It is always nice if your animal is able to remain with a single caretaker and in one home for the rest of its days. If you choose a caretaker who is likely to pass away before your animal, your animal will likely have to be re-homed again. Of course, this is still better than going to a shelter, but there is a certain amount of disruption and stress anytime there is a change or transition.

Thus, it is best to take as many steps as you can to make sure your initial caretaker will be able to give your animal a loving home for the rest of its life. Selecting a caretaker that is expected to outlive your animal is one of the easiest steps you can take, particularly if you have a short-lived animal.

Long-Lived Animals

It is absolutely imperative to put a plan in place if you own an animal with a lifespan longer than your own. The probability is very high that you will die before your animal, and without a plan in place, your animal will be left if a very dangerous limbo. Planning is crucial.

In cases where animals are very long-lived, tortoises, for example, your plan must also be sure not to violate the rule against perpetuities (RAP). RAP is a concept that many attorneys do not even fully understand, however if you have a long-lived animal, it is very important that you find one who does. Suffice it to say, RAP says that if you're going to give something to someone, then you must do it within a certain period of time. When planning for a long-lived animal, it is important to make sure that your plan doesn't violate the time periods established by RAP. This is just another reason why selecting a competent attorney that you enjoy working with is essential.

If you are the owner of a long-lived animal it is crucial that you put a plan in place for its uninterrupted care. It is highly likely that the animal will outlive you, and your plan must guarantee that your animal is protected for the duration of its life.

Also, with long-lived animals, it is more likely that your animal will not remain with a single caretaker for the rest of its life. It may be necessary for that animal to be transitioned to one or more back-up caregivers after the initial caregiver, so it's really important to make sure you have good back-ups. It is also imperative that you make plans with an organization of last resort, again because with long-lived animals there is a greater probability you will need one. The good news is that there are often species-specific organizations that serve as sanctuaries for these types of animals.

If you have a long-lived animal, planning for them may require a bit more foresight, but planning it is still very straightforward and absolutely critical. The provisions for your ACT can be tailored specifically to your animal's needs, and the basic components are still the same. You will create an ACT, appoint trustees and caretakers, and provide the necessary instructions to create a comprehensive system of checks and balances that guarantees your animal is protected.

Common Animals

Dogs and cats are by far some of the most popular companion animals in the world today, which also makes them the most common. Given their popularity, it follows that a larger percentage of people are familiar with the needs of caring for these animals. This is a good thing. It means that it will be easier for you to select a caregiver that is familiar with caring for your animal.

Because most people know how to care for a cat or a dog, your animal care instructions can be very simple and do not need to include a lot of detail. You may prefer to add more information to guide your caretakers, but it won't be absolutely imperative. If you have a cat or a dog it will be a very straightforward process to plan for your animal. Meaning, there's NO excuse not to do it. You don't want your animal to end up like poor Twink from the beginning of this book.

Your overall plan will include an ACT, and you will select the appropriate individuals to serve as your trustee, caretaker, and trust protector. You will also name two to three back-ups for each of these positions. You will include your animal care instructions, possibly an ACA, and you will name your final beneficiaries. You will transfer your property into your trust, and voila, you have responsibly planned to protect yourself, your estate, your loved ones, and of course, your animal.

Planning for your dog and/or cat is a simple process, and it is absolutely essential that you do it. The common nature of these animals comes with a downside as well. The number of unwanted dogs and cats in the world increases exponentially each year, and a simple plan is the only way to guarantee your animal is not one of them.

Exotic & Special-Needs Animals

Exotic animals includes all types of animals other than your usual household animals (i.e. cats and dogs), including birds, tortoises, reptiles, fish, etc. Most people are not familiar with the requirements of caring for these animals, and you need to be aware of this when putting together your plan. It may be more difficult to select appropriate caregivers because not everyone knows how to take care of tortoises, parrots, or other types of exotic animals and fish.

Special-needs animals are also animals that require very specialized care that most people will not be familiar with. Caring for these animals will take a special person who understands the particular needs of your animal.

Caregiver selection is of the utmost importance when it comes to exotic or special-needs animals. It is essential to select caregivers who are familiar with your animal, and have the skill-set necessary to care for it.

Your caregiver instructions are also critical, and should be quite comprehensive in either of these cases. You want to set your caretaker up for success, so that your animal is happy. Include as many details as possible, and give your caretaker as many "trial runs" as possible. Meaning, when you go out of town for a few days, let them take care of your animal to make sure they are up to the task.

With exotic and special needs animals, your successor trustees will also need to pay a bit closer attention to make sure that your animal is being properly cared for.

All in all, planning for an exotic or special-needs animal is no more complicated than planning for any other animal. However, it is even more critical that you have a plan. These types of animals are the most difficult to find homes for, and often meet tragic ends without the proper planning.

Horses

Horses are very popular, and there are a lot of people who have them. Some horses live a very simple life and require very little. Others may be competitive show horses with an entire cadre of people responsible for their care. It is also not unusual to see horses that are a bit of both, depending on what stage of life they are in. Regardless, when planning for a horse, there are some added layers of complexity that may come into play.

For example, horses are abnormally expensive. Meaning the horse itself costs a lot of money, and feeding and caring for it does as well. If you have a competitive show horse, all of those expenses will start to increase exponentially. Your plan *must* include the money necessary to provide the expected level of care for your horse. Also, because of their intrinsic value, horses are at a higher risk of being sold for money, including to kill-buyers who send them to slaughter. Once you realize and understand that your horse may just be dollar signs to some people, your plan can be drafted to protect against this. Money is an important factor to consider from all angles when planning for a horse.

Horses are also dangerous animals if for no other reason than their size. If you don't know what you're doing around horses, either you or the horse could easily wind up seriously or fatally injured. So, it is incredibly important to choose the right caretakers. It is essential that they be experienced horse-people, who truly love and understand horses. It may also be appropriate to establish a team of professionals that are available to assist the caretaker with the day-to-day responsibilities of caring for your horse. This team would be overseen by the primary caretaker, and might include a trainer, rider, vet, farrier, chiropractor, etc. The idea here is to create a plan that allows your horse's regular care to continue uninterrupted, whatever care that might be.

Horses are also not generally accepted at most animal rescues. Thus, it is imperative for you to select an organization of last resort where your horse can safely live for the rest of its life. Again, because of the expense, be prepared to make a financial contribution to the organization you select. All too often, old horses who have provided years of service find themselves being cruelly transported across the border to Mexico for slaughter. This is a heartbreaking end for any animal, and it can easily be avoided.

If you have a horse, you really need a plan.

Planning for a horse may seem more complicated than other animals, but this doesn't have to be the case. The ACT gives you the flexibility you need to make your plan as simple or complex as the situation calls for. You will appoint trustees and caretakers, provide them with your instructions, and perhaps establish a team of professionals to work with and provide support to the caretaker. Most importantly with horses, it is crucial that you do not forget about the money. You MUST set aside the money that will be needed for the care of your horse. Horses are expensive, and failing to provide the funds necessary to care for them is a surefire way to put their future in jeopardy.

Animals & the Law Today

Animals may be property under the law, but the ability to protect your animal, using an ACT is truly a blessing to animal owners. It is a legal tool that has not always been available to us, and we should be very thankful that there is now a legally binding way to plan for and protect our beloved animals. Don't take it for granted. Use it and take full advantage of all of its benefits.

The law is constantly evolving, and it has not always provided protection for our animals. As an animal lover, it is important for you to understand the legal landscape facing animals, not only to plan for and protect your own animals, but also to ensure all animals experience a high quality of life.

Did you know that up until the early 1900s animals were considered so worthless that they weren't even considered property? You could kill, maim, or torture an animal without any legal repercussions. Being considered property was actually a big step-up for animals, but we still need to do better.

Animals are not property, they are not commodities. They are alive with hearts and souls. They feel happiness, sadness, and yes, pain. They form strong families, and they love their families just as much as we love ours. These are not the characteristics of property. Property, like your car, your television, and your phone, does not love you back, but your animal does.

I am happy to report that the legal landscape for animals is changing every day, and the vast majority of that change is a really good thing for animals. There are great organizations, like the Animal Legal Defense Fund, working very hard to make sure all animals are protected under our laws and have a voice. Their work is a crucial part of effecting lasting change for animals.

There was a time when people were also treated like property: women were considered the property of their husbands, and slaves were considered the property of their masters. Thankfully treating humans as property is now illegal in this country and throughout the world. Humans are animals too, and it's time we extend that basic right to all animals. It is my hope that there will be a time when we look back on the way we have treated animals with the same disgust and horror that we now have for slavery or women being considered property.

Treating animals as property doesn't just have implications when it comes to estate planning. For example, if someone accidentally kills your cat or dog in front of you, they would only have to compensate you the value of the animal. Since there are so many cats and dogs in the world, the law attributes very little value to them, and you would receive nominal monetary damages, if any. You certainly would not receive anything for your emotional distress and suffering because an animal is just property. The flipside is if you witness someone accidentally kill a person, you would receive damages for emotional distress and suffering.

There was a recent case where a maid service accidentally let a family's dog outside and the dog was hit by a car. The maid put the dead dog under the dining room table and didn't even leave a note for the family. Traditionally, this family would have little or no recourse in this situation. Perhaps, they would receive a small sum for the value of the dog. However, in this case, the court awarded the family $65,000 in emotional distress damages, one of the largest in history. Animals may still be considered property under the law, but court decisions like this are an indicator that this may not always be the case.

Other signs of change can be found in recent legislation that the United States government has passed called the Pets Evacuation and Transportation Standards Act. This law requires emergency responders and rescuers to save pets as well as people during a natural disaster. That's a huge step in the right direction. Also, quick sidebar, I am only using the word "pet" here because it is the terminology used in the legislation. I have intentionally not used this term throughout this book because these animals are so much more than something you pet, and in my opinion calling them "pets" minimizes what they truly are.

Animal cruelty laws are also being updated and enforced with a new vigor. For example, the Federal Bureau of Investigation recently upgraded animal cruelty to a Class A felony. This means animal abusers are now in the same category as murderers. Animal cruelty crimes will now be a top priority for law enforcement and prosecutors. The message is spreading that animal cruelty is a very serious crime that will not be tolerated, and will be prosecuted to the maximum extent under the law. Perhaps one reason the FBI is treating animal cruelty crimes so seriously is because of the known correlation between serial killers and animal cruelty. Violence against animals, leads to violence against humans as well.

Strict animal cruelty laws are now prevalent in all states, but the problem is that they only protect cats and dogs. This leaves all other animals at risk, and sadly, there is still rampant animal cruelty facing these animals. Many animals, including dogs and cats, are suffering in commercial laboratories engaged in animal experimentation, testing, and vivisection. The animal cruelty laws do not apply to these labs, and they are free to abuse animals in the name of the almighty dollar. These animals spend what little life they have in a cage in a lab. They don't even get to go outside. This is completely unnecessary in today's world. There are many alternative ways to test products that don't involve abusing an animal. Thankfully, this too is changing, as more and more companies pride themselves on not testing or experimenting on animals.

Unfortunately, one of the biggest animal abusers is the meat and dairy industry in the form of factory farming. Fortunately, there is also a tremendous effort to end the cruelty animals experience in the factory farming industry, where these animals are truly nothing more than a way to make money. The large agriculture corporations will engage in any practice that saves them a dollar regardless of the impact on the animal.

This abuse and cruelty is finally being exposed thanks to the bravery of many undercover investigators. For decades, factory farms have been able to keep their disgusting practices concealed behind closed doors. They have even been successful at restricting your First Amendment right to free speech in the form of "ag-gag" laws.

An "ag-gag" law imposes fines and penalties on anyone who exposes the practices of a commercial farm. They punish whistleblowers, and have an incredibly chilling effect on reports of animal cruelty. Ag-gag laws still exist in many states, and are always sponsored and paid for by the meat and dairy industry.

Ag-gag laws are truly reprehensible. No one would ever stand for these types of laws if we were talking about people. We would be outraged if child abusers or elder abusers were allowed to hide behind closed doors. We must be outraged anytime someone engaged in cruelty is allowed to hide behind our laws.

Cows, pigs, birds, rabbits, monkeys, horses, the list goes on and on. These are all intelligent, loving animals, and if you got to know them the same way you have your cat or dog, you would see there's no difference. They feel happiness, sadness, pain and suffering, and they love deeply. Cats and dogs are currently the most protected animals under the law, and we need to extend that same protection to all animals whether they are in our home, on a farm, or in a lab. We have to stop making illusory distinctions between different species of animals, including humans.

Our laws should recognize that animals are not property, but in fact are sentient beings that experience love, happiness, excitement, as well as pain and distress. The country of New Zealand has taken this step, and has amended their laws to legally recognize animals as sentient beings. This amendment also includes a ban on the use of animal testing for beauty products. It is truly wonderful to see a country make such a significant change to its laws. Now, it is up to us as animal lovers to make sure the United States is not only joining, but leading this movement to change the legal landscape for animals everywhere.

Animals are an important part of our world, and they need us to protect them. Animals don't speak the spoken word, so we have to make an extra effort to understand them and make sure their interests are protected. Much like children, animals rely on us to do the right thing and make the right choices.

Over 200 years ago there was a population of more than two million wild mustangs roaming the United States. Today, there are less than 32,000. Why? Money. The Bureau of Land Management, which is funded by your tax dollars, is given the task of "clearing" land for commercial interests, otherwise known as cattle ranchers who want to graze beef cattle on the land. This involves using low-flying helicopters to cruelly and inhumanely round-up the Mustangs and remove them. The stress causes many of the pregnant mares to abort their babies. It results in broken bones for some, and death for others. Families are forever torn apart. We are causing this needless pain and suffering. This is unacceptable, and we as a society should not tolerate it. There is always a humane way, and if it's too expensive, too bad. Animals should not pay the price with their suffering. In the end, it is all of us who suffer.

A wise man named Albert Einstein once said, "If a man aspires towards a righteous life, his first act of abstinence is from injury to animals." Until we stop the cruelty and violence that we propagate on animals, we cannot expect to have a peaceful, non-violent society. Violence against animals, leads to violence against humans.

In the meantime, stay informed and keep speaking up for the animals. The world is becoming a better place for all animals day-by-day, and you are a part of that positive change. Your love for animals does make a difference. You can also make a tremendous difference in the life of your own animal by doing everything you can to protect it. Without your love and protection, it can still be a cruel world.

What Happened to Twink?

Remember our friend, Twink? You might be wondering, "Whatever happened to that poor, old girl?"

Well, I couldn't very well include her in this book without finding out, so I decided to take matters into my own hands.

I visited the shelter and found out that the Twink was with the same woman for 12 years. When she passed away, the woman's family tried to take Twink in, but for some reason it didn't work out and they surrendered her to the shelter. Twink was at the shelter for over six months. Shelter staff loved her dearly, and told me how heartbreaking it was that no one wanted this little dog because she was too old. For those six months, she lived in a cold, concrete kennel, and spent her nights alone.

I am quite certain this is not what Twink's owner would have wanted. With the proper planning, Twink could have been spared her experience in the shelter. Don't let your animal end up like Twink, or worse. Be responsible and do the right thing: put a plan in place protect your animal.

By the way, Twink lives with me now.

The End.

www.ingramcontent.com/pod-product-compliance
Lightning Source LLC
Chambersburg PA
CBHW041358090426
42741CB00001B/11